Gerbils

Everything About
Purchase, Care,
and Nutrition

Engelbert Kötter

BARRON'S

Contents

44 Husbandry and Health Care

Extras

The Typical Gerbil

They're the stars of the rodent scene: Mongolian gerbils have risen in popularity in recent years, surpassing the traditional favorites among the small rodents. That comes as no surprise to anyone who has made their acquaintance, because gerbils are cute, friendly, and easy to care for—in short, they're ideal pets!

Little Rodents with Big Appeal

There's never a dull moment when gerbils move in with you. You'll spend hour after hour in front of their cage watching the lively antics of these little Mongolians. Children, of course, are naturally attracted to gerbils, but it is completely normal if you, as an adult, quickly succumb to the charms of these lively creatures, too.

Even their outward appearance is captivating. Although Mongolian gerbils look a bit like mice, their thick coat, furred tail with a bushy tip, and generally adorable appearance make them attractive even for people who are less than enthusiastic about "real" mice or rats.

Before Mongolian gerbils captured the hearts of their fans, they were kept primarily as laboratory animals in the United States. From here they traveled to Europe. They have been available in pet stores since the 1960s in this country, and since the mid-1980s in Germany. The many color varieties of the Mongolian gerbil that have appeared in recent years have increased their popularity even more.

Ideal Pets

When you get right down to it, though, it is the nature of the animals themselves that turns rodent lovers into gerbil enthusiasts. Agile, suitable for adults, lithe, odorless, hand tame, alert, child-friendly, lively, inquisitive, low maintenance, active, uncomplicated, trusting—this is how people describe their gerbils. There's good reason that Mongolian gerbils have become the favorite rodents of the pet world in just two decades.

Meet the Gerbil

When people talk about gerbils, then strictly speaking they mean the Mongolian gerbil, *Meriones unguiculatus*. In German, the word for gerbil is *Rennmaus*, literally "running mouse," which comes as no surprise to anyone who has ever watched these speedy little creatures. As for solving the riddle of the scientific name *Meriones unguiculatus*: "Meriones" was a mythological Greek warrior; "unguiculatus" comes from Latin and means

"clawed." Whenever these adorable little creatures have to defend their territory or their rank in the clan, then they display the highly belligerent nature described by their scientific name.

Gerbils and their relatives are grouped in the family Gerbillinae. The genus *Gerbillus* (38 species), for which the family is named, is found in Arabic-speaking countries, where small, jumping desert animals are called "yarbu." Latinized, this became "gerbo," "gerbille" in French, and "gerbil" in English.

Where and How Gerbils Live

The Mongolian gerbil is also known as the Mongolian desert gerbil. This name is misleading, though, because they are not desert dwellers, but rather steppe animals. This description is derived from their primary range, the semiarid steppe that lies north and east of the Gobi Desert. There they are found in southern Mongolia from the foothills of the Altai Mountains to northeastern China. The climate in that area is continental. In the summer it is dry and very hot, in winter dry and freezing cold. Only 10 to 20 inches (25 to 50 cm) of rain and snow fall there annually. In keeping with the climate, Mongolian gerbils are equally well adapted to both dry heat and cold. For instance, they can obtain water by metabolizing the fat contained in food and keep each other warm in well-insulated nests even when the ground is frozen. The furred soles

Hello, friend! Standing up on their hind feet, gerbils check out their surroundings.

of their hind feet protect them against heat as well as cold.

Their steppe habitat is characterized by fine-grained limestone soil. About three-fourths of the land is covered with vegetation, mainly grasses and other herbaceous plants, with a scattering of shrubs. The gerbils feed primarily on the seeds of these plants.

Gerbils have a large abdominal scent gland (easily recognizable as a bald spot on their belly). They use the gland's secretion to mark their territory by rubbing their belly over rocks or plants. You can often see this marking behavior in your gerbils, for instance during out-of-cage time.

Martens and owls are the nimble gerbils' main predators.

Gerbil burrows: In the steppes, these agile rodents, which measure an average of 4 inches (10 cm) in length (without tail), construct their burrows underground: long tunnels about 1 to 1.5 inches (3 to 4 cm) in diameter, combined with an assortment of roomy chambers varying in size from as small as a mouse to as big as a bucket. The underground burrows are about 10 feet (3 m) in diameter and extend down to a depth of about 3 feet (1 m). They are often found in the dense root system of Siberian Peashrubs (*Caragana arborescens*).

Researchers have found three types of burrows. The simplest is a 3-foot-long (1 m) tunnel with two entrances, used as a temporary or escape burrow. A second type, the so-called summer burrow, is a tunnel system with about five to ten entrances and a nest chamber. The winter burrow has easily twice as many entrances, is branched, and also contains a food storage chamber for seeds of grasses and other herbaceous plants.

A wild-colored gerbil tries to find cover. The animal's need for safety and her curiosity appear to be in conflict with each other.

A Bit of **Systematics**

GERBILS Although their name in German (*Rennmaus*) literally means "running mouse," gerbils and mice are not closely related. Gerbils are rodents (Order: Rodentia) and belong to the same family as rats and mice (Muridae), but they are members of the gerbil subfamily (Gerbillinae) rather than the subfamily of Old World rats and mice (Murinae). In systematics, they have the same rank as hamsters (Cricetinae) or lemmings and voles (Arvicolinae).

JUMPING MICE Although Mongolian gerbils are sometimes mistakenly called "desert jumping mice," systematics makes it clear that these two groups are not closely related, either: Jumping mice belong to a separate family (Dipodidae), which is equal in rank to the Muridae.

Social structure Gerbils are territorial and live in family groups consisting of a dominant pair and their offspring from one or two litters. In groups like this, usually only the dominant pair breeds.

The family groups include both adults and juveniles. Family members recognize each other primarily by scent. In order for gerbils to tell if they've come face-to-face with a clan member or a territorial intruder, they quickly check each other's scent at every encounter. Gerbils groom each other's fur, and in the process they exchange special secretions with their saliva that serve as a recognition scent. If a gerbil has no contact with clan members for only two or three days and thus gets no "booster scent," she is no longer recognized as a clan member and will be attacked and bitten as a stranger. The animals also recognize each other by their urine.

The tail is an important part of the gerbil's body when it comes to maintaining balance in shaky situations.

Lively Social Animals

Gerbils in a family group live in close contact: They lie in a disorderly heap in the nest, sometimes piled three deep. Older sisters act as foster mothers to help rear the young. But things aren't always peaceful. As the clan gets larger (especially when there are more than 20 animals), squabbles break out over rank in the social hierarchy. These can be initiated by the dominant animals, but also by competing juveniles. Usually the highest ranking pair bites and drives away the weakest males and the strong, competing females. Thus clans split up and new ones are established. This natural behavior explains why there can be problems when introducing unfamiliar gerbils to each other (see page 42) and why escalating battles sometimes occur in an apparently established group (see page 43).

Well-developed Sense Organs

Ears: Gerbils have extremely sensitive ears. They can hear sounds with frequencies from 200 to over 32,000 hertz. In comparison, we humans hear frequencies ranging from 16 to 20,000 hertz, the best being at our "normal speech" frequency between 2,000 and 5,000 hertz. This means gerbils hear higher-pitched sounds better than humans; they can even detect the ultrasonic cries made by bats (20,000 to 50,000 hertz). That explains why pet gerbils are sensitive to noises like loud music and to ultrasonic frequencies (over 20,000 hertz) inaudible to human ears, like those emitted by televisions or computers (see page 23). Gerbil pups, in particular, use ultrasonic squeaks to call to their mother.

As with humans, the ability to hear changes with age in gerbils. Older animals hear best at a frequency of about 4,000 hertz, younger ones around 15,000 hertz.

Gerbils are anything but loners. Physical contact with others of their kind gives the animals a sense of security and well-being.

Fastidious creatures, gerbils groom themselves frequently. To do this, they sit on their hind legs and start cleaning their coat with their front paws.

When there's danger, gerbils drum with their hind legs. These sound waves quickly reach nearby animals as well as those some distance away. In addition, the drumming sounds are transmitted by the ground. This way gerbils can tell from which direction they come.

Whiskers: The whiskers (tactile hairs) on the animal's head are also direction finders. At even the slightest touch, each whisker acts like a long lever, stimulating the nerve cells located at its base. This way the animal can easily determine the diameter of a tunnel in the burrow, the width of a narrow hiding place, or the size of an object suddenly appearing within whisker range.

Eyes: Depth perception is not very well developed in gerbils. While their protruding eyes allow them a nearly panoramic view, the visual fields of the two eyes barely overlap—too little for three-dimensional vision like that we humans possess. The gerbil compensates for this with a trick: She

stands up on her hind legs, moves her head up and down when examining an object, and compares the two different images that result. Since a nearby object moves past the eye faster than one that is farther away, the gerbil knows that if she has moved her head only slightly and the two images differ from each other, then the object is close. The more she has moved her head, the more distant the object.

Sense of direction: Gerbils can guess the direction of movement better than humans. For instance, when they see another gerbil running, they don't run to the same spot. Instead, they dart immediately to the place where their paths will probably intersect. That requires the little rodents to be extremely good at spatial reasoning. And, in fact, when the animals are in danger, they don't retrace their route back to their burrow, but instead quickly return by the shortest "calculated" path.

Anatomy and Senses

Eyes

For gerbils in the wild, enemies are lurking everywhere. Their protruding eyes, located on either side of the head, give them an especially large field of vision. With this "panoramic view," the animals can even spot approaching birds of prey without constantly having to look overhead. However, their depth perception is very poor because the visual fields of the two eyes barely overlap.

Nose

The internal surface of the gerbil's nose is more densely packed with olfactory cells than that of humans. This is essential because gerbils use an olfactory language—incomprehensible to us—in which different scents each have their own specific meaning.

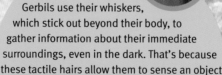

Whiskers

Gerbils use their whiskers, which stick out beyond their body, to gather information about their immediate surroundings, even in the dark. That's because these tactile hairs allow them to sense an object or the diameter of passageways or tunnels even before they touch it with their body.

Ears

You can hear your gerbils squeak, but not growl. That's because their vocalizations are primarily in the high-frequency range. The gerbils' sensitive hearing is adapted to this. The animals can even detect sounds that are far beyond our own hearing range, such as those made by bats. Unfortunately, this also includes high-frequency sounds from electronic devices.

Incisors

The gerbil's chisel-like incisors, which grow continuously throughout life, are both tools and weapons. The animals love to gnaw on food as well as nesting material. The razor-sharp teeth can pierce the hide of an enemy—or sometimes the finger of an unfortunate owner if the normally friendly gerbil is feeling uncharacteristically aggressive.

Claws

The gerbil's well-developed claws, which give the animal its scientific name, are used in the wild for excavating extensive underground burrows as well as for self-defense.

Feet

If you look closely, you can see that the soles of the hind feet (top) are furred while those of the front feet (bottom) are naked. The advantage of this is that the hind feet are better protected against the rugged terrain of the steppe, which is hot in summer and cold in winter, and the hairless front paws are better for grasping.

Gerbils as Pets

If you fell in love with gerbils at first sight, that's wonderful. However, don't be too quick to decide on getting gerbils without giving it careful consideration. Make sure you understand exactly what the purchase will mean for you and your family.

Are Gerbils Right for Me?

Children are not the only ones who are fascinated by gerbils. These agile rodents quickly captivate grown-ups as well. While children are primarily attracted by the adorable appearance of their gerbils, teenagers and adults soon discover the many different types of behavior shown by these steppe dwellers. Of course, gerbils will only be friendly when it suits them. Although these little pocket pets may tempt you to try carrying them, they will immediately start squirming around and want to get down from your hand. That's only natural: Even spontaneous meetings between gerbils are usually brief. For this reason, the best way to enjoy the friendliness of these animals is to let gerbils be gerbils and enjoy it when, as an occasional highlight, they voluntarily crawl onto your hand.

> Gerbils do not have an unpleasant odor if they are cared for properly (see page 50). That distinguishes them from animals like mice.
> Gerbils are easy to keep. They just need fresh food and chewable material daily. You should remove the obvious dirt once a week and clean the cage once a month. Let them out of the cage once a week for exercise. You can even give them enough food and water to last for a few days, and then they can stay alone when you want to go away, say for a long weekend.
> If you'll be gone for a week or more, then to be on the safe side it's a good idea to ask someone who is familiar with gerbils to take care of the animals or at least to check on them properly.
> Gerbils need a roomy cage and never like to be kept singly. Do you have space for this?

As with this free-roaming animal, Mongolian gerbils voluntarily make contact with people, even if it is usually for just a moment.

> The cost of keeping gerbils will increase if you breed them and when it's time to visit the veterinarian. Are you prepared to pay for this?

> Consider beforehand whether you or a member of your family has an allergy that could cause problems if you get a gerbil (for instance, an allergy to animal dander, straw, hay, or peanuts).

> Gerbils are active during the day (diurnal) and at night (nocturnal). They spend the day in a sleep-wake rhythm of cycles lasting about two to four hours each. Thus, you can rouse the little rodents at any time—they'll be wide awake instantly! That makes them more attractive for schoolchildren than pets like the nocturnal golden hamster. On the other hand, even people who work evening and night shifts will find a lively pet waiting for them when they return home. Bear in mind, though, that because of the animals' nocturnal antics, bedrooms (for example, the children's room) are not suitable locations for the cage.

> Their average life expectancy is about two and one-half to three and one-half years. Occasionally a Mongolian gerbil will even live to be five to six years old.

Gerbils and Children

Children can keep gerbils once they reach school age. This way they learn to assume responsibility. Until they are about ten years old, they need adult supervision to do this successfully for any length of time. As they get older, children can then assume full responsibility for taking care of the animals.

Gerbils and Other Pets

TIPS FROM
GERBIL EXPERT
Engelbert Kötter

It is not a good idea to house gerbils together with other pets:

CATS They hunt Mongolian gerbils. On the other hand, there was a report of one extremely aggressive gerbil that wasn't afraid to attack a cat.

RABBITS AND GUINEA PIGS Keeping gerbils with these pets, which tend to be rather peaceable, is not a good idea because they have very different requirements for cage design, diet, and activity times.

HAMSTERS, (FANCY) MICE, RATS Housing gerbils with other small rodents or even with other gerbil species often ends in bloody fighting and biting.

BIRDS It is not a good idea to keep gerbils on the bottom of aviaries, where they would be expected to eat bird food that falls on the floor. This is unsuitable not only because of the bird droppings, but also because they can be preyed upon by gerbil-hunting birds, such as parrots.

Gerbils in Portrait

Mongolian gerbils are anything but drab. They now come in about 40 interesting color varieties. You can buy some of them in pet stores; others are available from gerbil breeders.

DARK EYED HONEY Sandy-colored gerbils with a light underside are called Dark Eyed Honey, or simply DEH.

BLACK Black gerbils are glossy beauties, but rarely are they completely black: the bib and paws are often white. Dull black is called Slate. These varieties are now widely available in pet stores.

AGOUTI This is how breeders describe wild-colored gerbils. The coat color develops when the base of each hair is light, the middle is brown, and the tip is black. The resulting "three-colored" hair creates the impression of this color.

SIAMESE In Siamese gerbils, certain parts of the coat are more heavily pigmented than others; Burmese are similar but darker in color.

SPOTTED There are different types of spotted gerbils, including Spotted Agouti and Spotted Black. They look very lively, especially when they dash around during out-of-cage time.

LILAC The color variety Lilac is very elegant. It occurs when a particular gene lightens the dark coat in animals that would otherwise be black.

BURMESE Burmese (also known as Colorpoint Black) is the term for gerbils in which the nose, paws, and tail are darker in color than the rest of the coat.

DARK TAILED WHITE Despite their white coat and red eyes, Dark Tailed White (or Himalayan) gerbils are not true albinos. Distinguishing characteristic: In older animals, the hair of the tail turns grayish.

Gerbil Watching

With their wide range of behaviors and special senses, gerbils tempt us to spend many delightful hours in their company. I can assure you that, even after many years, life with gerbils is never dull.

Interesting Observations

As soon as you arrive home with your newly purchased gerbils, it is interesting to watch how they gradually take over their new cage. They display their full behavioral repertoire as they begin to explore, sniff, mark their territory with their abdominal scent gland (see page 7), clear trails for themselves with their teeth, and dig here and there in the bedding or nesting material. It is also exciting to watch the social behavior of gerbils toward each other. Each time they meet, they sniff each other briefly, then continue exploring on their own. If a gerbil finds a tasty treat while searching for food, she disappears with it into one corner of the cage in order to enjoy it all to herself.

When she does this, she frequently turns her back to the other gerbils. If another animal still tries

They live in family groups themselves and are "family pets": Grown-ups buy gerbils for the children, but soon find that they, too, are just as fascinated by these lively creatures.

to get at the tidbit, the feasting gerbil turns away and delivers a few smacks with her front paws, accompanied by defensive squeaking at very high frequencies. Test this yourself with a sunflower seed or a peanut!

Orientation: During their exploratory rambles in their cage or when roaming free outside, the animals use the organ of balance (vestibular apparatus) in the inner ear to register both the direction as well as the distance they have traveled. This helps them find the shortest path back to their burrow in the wild, or the way to the open door of their cage during out-of-cage time (see page 36).

Alarm: Drum like a gerbil on the floor when the animals are roaming free, or on a tabletop when the gerbils are in the cage. As if on command, they disappear instantly into their burrow; that's because drumming with their hind legs is how the little rodents warn each other of danger. The inquisitive creatures don't stay under cover for long, though, but instead peek out alertly again within seconds.

Activities: In the wild, the animals spend most of their time foraging for food. For this reason, when you keep gerbils as pets it is important to put their food on the bedding and not in a bowl (see page 48). This way they can keep themselves

busy by digging for it. Because these agile rodents eat their fill relatively quickly, they need new stimuli to keep them happy: for example, an enriched cage environment (see page 23) and a wide assortment of chewables (see page 28).

Gerbils also climb a little—at least they quickly master climbing to different levels of the cage (see page 34). When they do this, the tail, which is as long as the body, plays an important role in maintaining balance. Holding a gerbil in your hand, turn her onto her back, then watch how she uses her tail to gain momentum in order to roll back onto her feet.

Gerbils are good climbers but are a little unsure of themselves on toys that are too narrow, like this rope.

Living with Gerbils

Mongolian gerbils are comparatively easy to keep. However, they are by no means undemanding. What they ask of their owner is a home with plenty of activities so that they don't get bored. To care for this species properly, you need to provide outlets for their agility and curiosity.

Buyer Be Aware

When you decide on Mongolian gerbils, you'll be getting pets that are remarkably agile, lively, and inquisitive, yet at the same time relatively trusting. Spending time with them will quickly become a normal part of your daily routine. This lets you check on the animals regularly without having to schedule extra time for it.

But First, a Request

Before you set out to buy your gerbils, think over your decision one last time. Experience has shown that it makes sense not to be too hasty when buying gerbils: Genuine enthusiasm for gerbils will last. This is especially true when children express a desire for these lively Mongolians; you should feel free to spend a few days deliberating and making plans with them in order to find their real reasons for wanting a pet. A movie or comic strip about animals should not be the trigger—gerbils are living creatures! Boredom or a lack of contact with children their own age should not be the deciding factor, either—gerbils certainly keep a child busy, but they can never be a substitute for a human playmate. However, gerbils can help shy children become less withdrawn, because the animals actively approach their owners.

If you and your children plan the purchase of Mongolian gerbils together, then agree on which responsibilities they'll have for their new companions. On page 50 you'll find a list of chores required in caring for gerbils. You and your children should make a note of these in your daily schedule.

Decisions, Decisions

When you're deciding on which gerbils to buy, the age and sex of the animals play a role. You can get young gerbils that are about eight to twelve weeks old. The young ("pups") should not be separated from the group sooner than seven or eight weeks after birth, because around this time they learn and express their social behavior. The advantage of young animals is that you know just how old they are when you get them. That helps you make a realistic estimate of how long they are likely to live (see page 13).

You can find how to recognize a healthy gerbil in the Checklist on page 22.

1 The genitals of the female lie flat against the abdomen. The distance between anus and vagina is very small. Gerbil mothers have clearly recognizable nipples.

2 In males the scrotum (visible from the side) begins to bulge after about the eleventh week of age. Anus and genitals are clearly separated.

In practice, however, the very early age at which gerbils are sold often proves to be a pitfall because it is still difficult to determine their sex at that time. Even experienced owners frequently make "sorting errors," with the result that an owner who has purchased a same-sex pair of gerbils is astonished when they happen to reproduce unexpectedly. If you want to be sure you're buying two males, it's best to wait the additional one or two weeks until they are clearly distinguishable from the females.

Never Keep Just One Gerbil!

Always buy at least two animals. Gerbils are gregarious creatures with a definite need for social contact. A person cannot take the place of another gerbil.

In the long run, two males actually get along better than two females. Among the latter, fighting and biting occur relatively more often. In principle, a squabble over rank, in which both animals compete for dominance, can occur in animals of either sex. Ostracism of individual animals tends to occur more frequently in larger groups (from 10 to 20 animals).

Castration: I am frequently asked whether or not the male in a mixed-sex pair of gerbils should be castrated so that two animals known to get along can be kept together—without an abundance of offspring (see page 58). However, I advise against subjecting a gerbil to the stress of an operation. Anesthetizing a small rodent like the gerbil is especially difficult. Besides, not all gerbils survive this kind of surgery.

Where to Buy Gerbils

Once you have decided to buy your gerbils, you'll have no trouble finding suitable suppliers.

Pet stores: The traditional place to buy gerbils is the pet store. The dealer will give you tips on how to keep these steppe animals when you buy them. Pet stores also carry a large selection of suitable cages, accessories, and gerbil food, including live food (see page 46). If you are searching for particular color varieties of the Mongolian gerbil (see page 14), you'll be most likely to find what you're looking for in pet stores or hobbyist magazines (see addresses on page 62). This is also true if you are interested in other gerbil species.

Private individuals: There are always ads for Mongolian gerbils in daily newspapers and shopping guides as well as on bulletin boards at shopping centers and veterinary offices. Even kindergarten and school groups have gerbils to give away; these are usually surplus offspring of their own captive-bred animals. With all these possibilities, you have a good chance of getting young animals.

Wherever you go, though, take a good look at the owner, animals, and living conditions to make sure you get healthy, clean animals (see Checklist, page 22). It is especially important to get animals from a clean home if you already have gerbils and want to increase your stock by adding young animals. You may need to do that if, for example, you have one gerbil and would like to get another to keep him company (see page 42) or if you are looking for a suitable breeding partner (see page 58). Otherwise you will put your stock at risk. A gerbil owner whose own home is well cared for will certainly be able to provide healthy animals from a good environment.

Animal shelters: You can be certain that the gerbils from animal shelters are healthy and well cared for. In addition, when you get Mongolian gerbils from an animal shelter, you are supporting these establishments and also doing some good

Small cages like this one are great for transporting gerbils safely, and they are also useful when you are trying to introduce unfamiliar animals to each other.

for the animals themselves, because you can give them more time and attention than the busy staff at the shelter. Gerbils there are often given away with fairly complete cage setups, so rescuing "orphans" like these is not only good for the agile little creatures, but it also makes financial sense for you. If you are really enthusiastic about gerbils, then you should seriously consider taking the residents of animal shelters, especially if the age of the gerbils is not of primary importance for you.

Animal shelters give away both surplus youngsters as well as older gerbils. You can even leave a "pet wanted" ad at the shelter if you are looking for special animals, for instance, a certain age or a specific color variety (see page 14). The shelter can notify you if and when suitable animals are left there or are waiting to be adopted at another shelter in the region.

Health at a Glance

WHAT TO LOOK FOR	
EYES	They are wide open, clean, and clear. The animal appears alert, lively, and interested in the surroundings.
LEGS AND FEET	The limbs are intact, without injuries, and there are no improperly healed fractures. The nails are not overgrown or crooked.
COAT	It must be smooth, not scruffy, and should not have any bald spots. The abdominal gland does not count as a bald spot.
GENITAL AREA AND ANUS	Both are clean, with no sign of diarrhea or discharge.
WEIGHT	The adult gerbil is normal in size, neither emaciated (females obviously less than 2 ounces [60 g], males less than 2.5 ounces [70 g]), nor obese (females over 3.5 ounces [100 g], males over 3.8 [110 g]).
NOSE	It is dry and clean, with no discharge.
TEETH	The four incisors are shaped normally and do not wiggle around.
BEHAVIOR	The animal is lively and agile. After waking up, he is immediately alert, curious, and lively. He does not sit apathetically (with closed eyes) apart from the group.

Going Home

Your pet dealer will put your gerbils in a folding cardboard box, or you can buy a special travel carrier at the pet store (see photo, page 21). Take your pets home as quickly as possible. The noises made by your car are just as unpleasant for gerbils as the bumpy ride and changes in direction during the drive (see pages 8–9), which are confusing for the animals. You can reduce the stress of the trip home by cushioning the travel carrier on a blanket on the floor behind the passenger's seat. It will sit there securely and can't slide around or fall off the seat when you brake. If a passenger holds the carrier in his or her hands during the trip, then it will shake constantly! Pay attention to the existing temperature during the trip home, especially the difference between the air-conditioned pet store, where the temperature is optimal, and the outdoors. These steppe animals aren't bothered by dry, warm summer temperatures, but they don't like damp, cool weather. You have to protect the animals, which are sensitive to dampness, by placing the travel carrier on something like a hot-water bottle (lukewarm).

Cozy Quarters

Gerbils are agile animals interested in everything around them. To make sure that you enjoy these adorable critters (and they enjoy you!), start by housing them in a cage where they can express their natural behavior to the fullest extent possible.

The Right Location

› The cage should be located in a place that is quiet, well lit, dry (low humidity), and warm, with temperatures between 59° and 77°F (15° and 25°C). Don't place it in direct sun, otherwise you'll have to provide some means of shading it.

› Since gerbils are active both day and night, they're always making noise, for instance, when they race around on their exercise wheel. To ensure that you aren't bothered by this, don't set up the cage in a bedroom.

› The animals do not like to be disturbed by drafts, unpleasant smells, steamy kitchen fumes, tobacco smoke, loud music, or devices like televisions or computers that emit disturbing noises in the ultrasonic range (see pages 8–9). A cool, damp cellar is also unsuitable, even if it is well lit.

› If you keep the gerbils in a wire cage, you can't entirely prevent them from kicking bedding out of the cage with their constant burrowing and digging. While you can always vacuum this up from a rug or carpet, it can be difficult if the tiny wood fibers get caught in the fabric. A floor covering that can be swept clean with a broom is therefore an advantage.

Size: You can easily keep two gerbils in a cage with 3 square feet (0.3 m²) of floor space. For three to five gerbils, you need about 6 square feet (0.6 m²) of floor space, and about 10 square feet (0.9 m²) for up to nine animals.

How Gerbils Prefer to Live

When it comes to the design of suitable housing for gerbils, owners fall into two different camps: those who favor small animal cages, and those who prefer aquariums or terrariums ("gerbilariums").

Small animal cages: These consist of a plastic bottom tray and a wire top. Comfortable, larger models have several levels and even come with casters. When you buy a cage, check to see if the model you like can be opened from different sides and everything inside is within reach. The wire bars of the top should be no more than 0.5 inch (12 mm) apart so that pups cannot crawl between them.

For a gerbil, the most important "feature" of the perfect home is another gerbil. That's why you should always keep at least two gerbils.

A bottom tray with rounded corners is easier to clean than one with sharp corners. The tray should be relatively deep, because then you can put in a thick layer of bedding and the gerbils won't be able to kick much of it out with their vigorous digging.

Important: Gerbils will nibble on or chew up all plastic parts in no time! This means the cage must be sturdy enough so that the damaged plastic parts do not become a safety hazard. The door latch cannot be made of plastic, otherwise the little rascals will chew on it and be able to escape. Stay away from models that have a wire top that rests on special plastic supports rather than directly on the bottom tray. These will quickly be gnawed to bits! Then the top will slide into the tray, or else it will sit at an angle, leaving a gap at one end through which the animals can escape.

Glass tank: The advantage of this design, also known as a "gerbilarium," is that you can put in a deep layer of bedding, yet very little dirt escapes. It is also easy to clean if you remove the accessories and lay it on its side. The disadvantage, though, is that it is heavier and thus harder to handle; in addition, water bottles and other

With special tubes from the pet store, you can easily connect several cages to make a multiple-unit system. Make sure you check the plastic seals for signs of chewing, though, to prevent escapes!

accessories as well as built-in furnishings are more difficult to attach to a glass wall than a wire cage.

To keep the gerbils from jumping out of their cage—the animals can clear 16 inches (40 cm) easily—a glass tank must be tightly covered with a wire mesh top. A Plexiglas sheet is not suitable as a cover because any dust that is produced, for instance, when the gerbils dig, cannot escape, and dust can harm the eyes and respiratory organs of your little rodents (see page 55).

Glass tanks cost more than small animal cages made of plastic and wire.

Deluxe Gerbil Habitat

If you are handy, then you can create a multiple-unit cage system by combining several smaller cages using tubes, for example drainage pipe (from the home improvement center) at least 3 inches (8 cm) in diameter. To do this, bend the tubes into a U-shape and connect the cages with them. Attach the tubes to the roof of the cage with wire ties. The ends of the tubes should reach almost to the bedding so that the gerbils can climb into them easily. This way you'll create a system of cages that the gerbils will treat like their burrows in the wild. They'll have plenty of room to move around and can set up different living areas: They can make a nest area in one cage, an area for eating in another, and in a third a play area where they can either entertain themselves by digging, gnawing, and climbing or else busily gather nesting material and carry it through the connecting tunnels into the nest area. As you see, you can use your own ideas to create a habitat that will stimulate your gerbils' excellent spatial reasoning ability, well-developed senses, and boundless curiosity.

Additional levels increase the floor space of the cage considerably. The gerbils can easily reach them by climbing up the attached ramps.

Recommended Cage Accessories

Mongolian gerbils living in the wild have very special needs, which you must take into consideration when choosing the necessary cage accessories for your pets.

1 Exercise wheel

Free-standing wheels are best. Weigh down the base of a standard wheel with a ceramic tile so that it doesn't wobble or fall over when the gerbils race around on it. Wheels designed to be hung are difficult to attach in glass tanks, and in wire cages they transfer vibrations to the wire top, which is noisy and annoying. Make sure the exercise wheel you buy has a solid rear wall. Otherwise there's a risk that the gerbils will slip between the drum and the stand and catch their tail or break a leg. Metal exercise wheels are best because they can't be damaged by gnawing.

Tip: Not all gerbils take to exercise wheels. Some are crazy about them; others won't give them a second look. Imprinting in infancy seems to play a role here. Nevertheless, make one available.

2 Climbing toys

Climbable rocks, roots, or pieces of wood are all suitable. Pet stores carry a wide assortment of toys that you can give gerbils to keep them busy and to make their cage more interesting. Wood has proven to be the best material for this; gerbils will nibble on it and chew it up, but unlike plastic it cannot form sharp edges or be a health threat if they swallow slivers of it. Besides, plastic can contain toxic plasticizers.

3 Food bowl

This is primarily for fresh and live foods. Choose a material that cannot be damaged by chewing, such as ceramic. It's best to put dry food on the bedding, because it is more exciting for the animals to forage for it there than to have it served in a bowl. This helps to keep the animals busy. There's no merit to the objection that the food could be contaminated with droppings, because experience shows that gerbils defecate in their food bowls, too.

4 Bathing dish

Provide a dish (glass, ceramic) filled with chinchilla bath sand. The gerbils will roll in it, and this removes dirt from their coat.

5 Nesting material

Suitable nesting materials include anything that gerbils can shred with their teeth and use to build a nest ball, for example, hay, straw, napkins, paper towels or toilet paper ("tissue paper"). Pet stores also carry ready-made nest balls fashioned from natural materials.

6 Water bottle

Gravity-fed water bottles with sipper tubes (from the pet store) are best. The bottle must be cleaned thoroughly and filled with fresh water once a week. Even if the gerbils don't always drink the water (see page 48), you should still offer it.

Hiding Places

You don't have to give gerbils a conventional nest box, because they won't necessarily build their nest there. It is not even essential as a hiding place, because you'll certainly be providing the animals with plenty of toys that they can scramble over, climb on, crawl into, and hide in. The easiest option is to put cardboard boxes in the cage, like those used for rice, pasta, or cereal; cardboard rolls from paper towels or toilet paper are good, too.

Chewables

Gerbils spend a lot of time gnawing. For this reason, it is very important to provide gerbils with suitable chewable material in addition to "entertaining" toys (see page 35). There must always be plenty of it in the cage.

Experience has shown that gerbils are especially fond of gnawing on torn cardboard boxes, while corrugated cardboard is less popular. As far as branches are concerned (see page 29), fairly twiggy types are best for gnawing, especially those about 1/16 inch (1–2 mm) in diameter. It's best if you remove lightly gnawed, sturdier branches from the cage after two or three days, provided you don't want to leave them as a supporting framework for gerbil tunnels in and under the bedding (see page 35).

Tip: To help keep your pets busy, don't place all the "building materials" mentioned above right where they are to be used in the cage; instead, put them where the gerbils will have to carry them from one level to another.

The Right Bedding

The bedding in gerbil cages is different from that used for other small rodents. It gives the gerbils something to walk on, keeps the cage clean, serves as a place to play, and provides for activity. Bedding in the gerbil cage must give the animals an opportunity to dig. As in their native Mongolia, they like to excavate their burrows in it. For that reason, gerbils need a deep rather than a shallow layer of bedding.

While one curious pup emerges from the woven grass ball, a second explores the interior.

For many years, I have had success with the following combination of bedding materials: After cleaning the cage, I first cover the bottom with a layer about 3/4 to 1 inch (2 to 3 cm) deep of chinchilla bath sand from the pet store (play sand for sandboxes works, too). This is the bottom layer of bedding. The little critters can wear down their nails by scratching around in the sand (see page 56). For the top layer of bedding, I put in a little bit of chewable material every day. This could be a handful of hay and straw, paper towels and toilet paper ("tissue paper"), and even dry, lightly used napkins. Cardboard packaging and thin branches from fruit trees and other nontoxic woody plants (like hazelnut, birch, hornbeam) are also gradually gnawed up by the gerbils. Also popular are the thin slats of fruit crates from the supermarket; break them apart and remove any staples and nails before putting them in the cage. In time, your pets will chew all of it into bedding. Eventually, this layer will increase to a depth of 2 to 4 inches (5 to 10 cm), or 5 to 6 inches (12 to 15 cm) in a glass tank. Start by giving them primarily hay and straw, because after you have cleaned the cage, the first thing the gerbils have to do is rebuild their soft nest.

In a glass tank, the bedding should not get so deep that the animals can no longer stand upright in it and still have enough free room above their heads.

Important: Never give the animals synthetic bedding ("hamster fluff") as a substitute for hay and straw. This consists of fibers that can form snares. In the past, that has resulted in strangulated limbs or even necrosis of toes and paws, especially with young animals.

Considering how much these Asian acrobats love to chew, Mongolian gerbils might just as well be called Mongolian gnawers.

Is **Cat Litter** Necessary?

MASTERS OF THE DESERT Mongolian gerbils come from steppes and semidesert areas. Their bodily functions use water sparingly, so they produce only a little urine and very dry feces. For this reason, the top bedding does not have to be highly absorptive. The material described above will do a satisfactory job of absorbing what little moisture is produced.

PREVENTING ODOR BUILD UP If you like, you can still scatter a few handfuls of cat litter in the gerbil cage occasionally. The material has antibacterial as well as deodorant properties, although gerbils don't have an unpleasant odor anyway when cared for properly. It's best to get cat litter that is unscented, dust free, and contains no powder.

Acclimation Made Easy

Before you go to get your new pets, whether from the pet store or another source (see page 21), make sure you have everything at home prepared for their arrival; this way, after their upsetting trip in the travel carrier, the gerbils can move into their new quarters immediately. Be sure to check the temperature in the room once more; ideally it should be between 59 and 77°F (15 and 25°C) (see page 23). In any case, the little animals will fine-tune the temperature to meet their needs by opening or closing their nest. So that it doesn't

---

Schedule **for the First Few Days**

EVERYTHING IS NEW Let your gerbils have enough time to get used to their new home without being disturbed. The first thing they have to do is explore the cage and claim ownership by marking all new objects with their scent.

BREATHING SPELL Even if curiosity tempts you to do otherwise, make sure you and your children don't demand too much of the newcomers in the first few days. Give the animals the breather they need.

MAKING CONTACT Later on, your gerbils will come over to you at the side of their cage, voluntarily and increasingly often. This is how the animals signal that they would like you to come and "talk" to them. You can let your gerbils climb on you the first time they're allowed out of their cage to play.

---

get too hot for the animals in direct sunlight during the summer and around midday, they must be able to withdraw into a shady place in the cage. It's better if you can shade the gerbils with a venetian blind, a window shade, or a curtain. Albinos and other white color varieties of the Mongolian gerbil are especially sensitive to excessive exposure to the sun.

You're sure to have followed all the advice I gave on page 23 about choosing the right location. If you've put the cage in a spot you frequently walk by, you can always look in on your animals in passing to see how they're doing. I guarantee that you'll frequently catch yourself lingering there "for just a minute," fascinated by the gerbils and their lively antics.

Putting Them in the Cage Correctly

Transferring the gerbils is simple: As soon as you get home, place the opened travel carrier in the gerbil cage. The animals will then do the rest by themselves. If the transport carrier is a cardboard box, you can leave it in the cage; the animals will quickly gnaw it to bits. Alternatively, you can remove the box and save it to use as a suitable travel carrier whenever the need arises, for instance when you have to go to the veterinarian.

Tip: If you already have gerbils at home, then you should first house your new arrivals in a separate quarantine cage if you got them from private individuals. During the next four weeks, check the new arrivals for diseases. If they are healthy, you can put them in with your "stock." You'll find how to go about this on page 42.

Ever alert! Gerbils are active or in the nest in two- to four-hour cycles. That's why they need plenty of opportunity for activity.

Warm sand and soft, fragrant hay encourage the animals to take a break or, more often, a sand bath for coat care.

Getting Used to Each Other the Right Way

Your gerbils should first be allowed to become thoroughly familiar with their new surroundings and with you. This means that for the next three to four weeks they should stay in their cage without being disturbed. Only after this period can you begin to offer the gerbils new territory to explore by allowing them out of the cage to roam around freely.

Chores for children: You must also give yourself time to get used to your new companions. Children, especially, have to practice assuming some of the responsibilities, and these should at first be done under adult supervision. A list of gerbil care chores can be helpful in the beginning so that they get the hang of their daily, weekly, and monthly responsibilities. This way it quickly becomes a routine. You can also make the initiation to gerbil care easier for the children by tackling the necessary tasks together in a playful manner.

Keep in mind that children seek playful contact with their pets on their own, so to ensure that pets receive the necessary care they deserve, simply spend time with your children watching the gerbils to find out what the animals need, then encourage the children to meet these needs with loving care.

Tip: Explain to your children that gerbils are not the type of pets that are meant to be cuddled—even if they look adorable and make us want to pet them!

Gerbil-Friendly Taming

Gerbils become quite tame. You can read how to go about taming them in the boxes on page 33. However, you must learn to understand this tameness from the animals' point of view, because the human view of the same behavior or gesture can be unfairly contrary to that of the animal. Put yourself in the gerbil's place!

The animals are extraordinarily curious and therefore will keep coming up to you. As they do this, they will discover that they have nothing to fear from you, or better yet, that you have tasty treats for them. In this way they'll come to trust you. The gerbils' tameness is thus a combination of curiosity and trust. It does not mean that the animals submit to a person's will and, for example, obey commands like a dog. Instead, the tameness of gerbils is more like that of cats. Cats, too, have a mind of their own; they are as friendly as they want to be, whenever and however it suits them. To sum up: You must always use the animals' yardstick to measure tameness toward you as a human. At the same time, keep in mind that when gerbils make contact with each other, for example by sniffing, this contact is likewise brief, often lasting but a moment when they meet during their scouting trips around the cage. Even if a tame gerbil allows you to demonstrate your affection in gerbil fashion by scratching him behind the ear with your finger, that will never last for long. And it will never last as long nor be as intense as the communal snug-gling and grooming that goes on among gerbils in their nest!

Keep in mind that you are the more intelligent one. Taming, like training an animal, can only succeed when you take advantage of the animal's instincts. When you realize that, you will succeed in taming your gerbils in a way that shows respect for the animals.

However, that means not subscribing to the notion that "tame is when the gerbil does what I want, when I want." Instead, you should be saying to yourself: "I understand how a gerbil behaves. I am taking advantage of that in order to get as close as the animal will allow." Also keep in mind that gerbils have their own personalities, which means that some of them are more willing than others to make friends with people.

Winning Their Trust Step-by-Step

Taming a gerbil doesn't begin with the gerbil; on the contrary, it begins with you, or more precisely, with your careful observation of the animals. Many of the gerbils' behaviors are described in this manual. In order to understand these behaviors, try to spot them in your pets.

After that, begin with the next step. By observing your gerbils daily, you should be able to predict their reactions with a fair degree of accuracy. For instance, when a gerbil crawls out of his nest, the first thing he does is take a look around in the cage to discover "What's new!" And then he may run to the cage wires because he has found you there.

Be careful when handling a gerbil. He can suddenly jump out of your hand!

As soon as you have developed this sort of "feeling" for the gerbils, you are ready to take it a step further and begin to guide the animals. Perhaps you can use treats such as mealworms to tempt them to specific places—for instance onto your hand. If a gerbil tries to nip you, nudge him away gently but firmly. Nipping is a sort of test bite, as if to say, "How does that taste?" It doesn't always indicate aggression.

1 FIRST CONTACT Don't overwhelm the gerbils with your enthusiasm! Give them time to get used to your presence at the cage. Get to know the animals by watching them. A gerbil will quickly seek contact on his own and come to the side of the cage in order to sniff you.

2 GETTING USED TO YOUR HAND In the beginning, let them sniff your hands often through the cage wires. Then several times a day put your hand inside the cage so that the gerbils get used to it. They must learn that they have nothing to fear from your hand. Make sure that your hands are always scent free.

3 TEMPTING THEM ONTO YOUR HAND An open cage door is a temptation for the inquisitive animals. If they have grown accustomed to your hand in the cage, the gerbils will even scramble through the door onto your hand, especially if a treat awaits them there! When the animals eventually overcome their shyness and take the treats, you can try to pet them.

Providing Activities for Gerbils

For Mongolian gerbils, the day is subdivided in a sleep-wake rhythm of two- to four-hour cycles. In the wild, they spend up to 80 percent of their waking time foraging for food. In the cage they don't have to travel as far, and they eat their fill sooner, so they need other ways to stay busy.

Exploring and Climbing

Gerbils learn about their surroundings by exploring. In the cage, it doesn't take long for all nooks and crannies to be inspected, all scent marks placed, and all clan members checked out. Expand the range of activities available to your gerbils by giving them several different cage levels or even a multi-unit cage system with connecting tunnels (see page 25). The more animals you have in your clan, the more important this is, because it allows you to create ample space for a larger population in a smaller area. However, the total area should not exceed 11 square feet (1 m^2) for two animals, otherwise there's a danger that individual animals given too much space could come to regard each other as strangers because they'd meet less often and would no longer be able to keep reinforcing their scent recognition. This can lead to biting and fighting!

If you keep your gerbils in a fairly large cage—for example, one with 40 × 20 inches (100 × 50 cm) of floor space—then you can also install additional platforms at different levels in the cage. Wooden boards about 1/2 inch (15 mm) thick work well for this. Drill holes in the corners of the boards and attach them with wire to the roof of the cage. The gerbils can climb up to them using hanging bridges or rodent ramps and steps. Another useful toy is an exercise wheel. Please keep in mind the suggestions about this on page 26.

Climbing toys: Gerbils are not true climbers. Nonetheless they can clamber up ramps and short ladders with agility. Branches of suitable trees and shrubs (see page 29) are also an invitation to climb. However, gerbils will refuse complicated stunts like climbing ropes.

Digging and Hiding Games

The preferred location for these activities is at and below ground level. To keep your gerbils busy, it's best to provide sufficient bedding for burrowing (see page 28) rather than climbing toys; that's also true for mazes to crawl through, houses to play in

Gerbils will crawl into any available opening, then reappear after a brief investigation to survey their surroundings.

You have to replace plastic accessories, like this exercise wheel, once they succumb to the gerbils' sharp teeth.

Gerbils also like to investigate hollow blocks, but they prefer the shadowy interiors of tubes and tunnels to open toys like these.

(pet store), or dishes for sand baths (see page 26). You'll provide even more opportunities for fun if you give them tubes and hiding places in the cage. Place an empty cardboard box, for instance, a cereal box with the top torn off, on the bottom layer of bedding. Use tubes to make two passageways that end in the box. Cover the structure loosely with twigs (see page 29), hay or straw, and tissue. The gerbils will quickly commandeer this artificial burrow for themselves. If they want to use it, they will carry their nest into it; if not, then they will chew it into bedding and build their nest in a more suitable spot. They will also crawl among the twigs and shred many of them. The sturdier twigs that remain will provide a framework with empty spaces that can stay buried beneath the top layer of shredded bedding. This way the gerbils can create a burrow for themselves. Without a framework of this kind, they wouldn't be able to tunnel through the loose bedding and excavate passageways or nest chambers. However, this sort of structure should be restricted to one area of the cage or one-half of the floor space so that the gerbils still have enough room to move around. Only in a multiunit cage system (see page 25) can you allow it to take up one entire cage.

Suitable **Materials** in the Cage

TOYS Untreated wood and clean cardboard boxes have proven to be good. The fragments that result from chewing are used for bedding. Plastic is less suitable for gerbil accessories.

CAGE ACCESSORIES Anything you don't want to have destroyed by chewing should be made of metal, ceramic, or porcelain.

Playgrounds and Out-of-Cage Time

A spacious gerbil cage certainly provides these adorable rodents with enough room to romp around for weeks at a time and enjoy a variety of activities. Nevertheless, the first time you let your animals out of their cage to roam around freely, you will discover that there's a difference between their agility inside the cage and their exuberance outside it.

You will also see what an amazingly well-developed sense of direction and spatial reasoning ability Mongolian gerbils have (see page 9). All the same, give the gerbils a restricted exercise area, but one that's as large as possible, because then you will be better able to keep an eye on everything. If you let the speedy little creatures run around in an open area like a hallway, but not in a fully furnished living room, they can't get into any trouble or endanger themselves (see page 40).

Gerbil Playpen

As an alternative to free roaming, you can make an enclosed area for the gerbils in which you set up all kinds of toys, a sort of playpen (see page 38). Smooth wooden or plastic boards at least 20 inches (50 cm) high make suitable walls. Naturally, the gerbils don't think of cardboard boxes, wooden blocks, twigs, or roots as toys, but rather tunnels and cavities they can explore and crawl through. The animals will be happier if you place their "toys" closer to the walls, because they feel more secure there. If they are startled, for example, they will always run to the edge of the area and look for a protective hiding place there. Out-of-cage time will certainly be more fun for the gerbils if you participate actively yourself. Simply sit on the floor, then the gerbils will even include you in their hijinks!

Of course, that happens in gerbil fashion, like their encounters with other gerbils: approach slowly and cautiously, sniff briefly, everything's OK—and then dash away with tail held high. In time, the gerbils will investigate your pants leg

Gerbils climb ladders like this with ease—especially if tasty food or new territory to explore tempts them up.

as a hiding place. They will even climb on you and your clothes, stay with you for a while, and then take off for another adventure elsewhere. Watch out, though, that while your are being "overrun" the animals don't chew holes in your clothing!

Back to the House!

You can always tempt the little vagabonds to come back to you and even get tame animals to climb on your hand if you offer them a treat, perhaps a peanut, a sunflower seed, or best of all a meal-worm. This high point of your holiday outing is an ideal moment to pick up the vacationers and return them to their cage without frightening them. That way you don't have to shoo them into the cage, something you should avoid anyway lest you scare them and destroy their trust in you after you worked so hard to win it. To put an animal that you're holding back in the cage, carefully cover him with your other hand so that he can't jump out. You can also gently hold him by the base of his tail. Never grab a gerbil by the tail, though (see page 41). You can also outwit the gerbils by laying a card-board tube (mailing tube) on the floor. As soon as the inquisitive animals come over to investigate it and crawl inside, hold both exits closed and trans-fer the little critters to the cage. You could also put the cage, with its door open and entry ramp in place, inside the enclosed area. Then when the gerbils are hungry, curious, or tired, they can climb in by themselves. You still have to shut the cage door right away, though, because the gerbils will

Have fun together when your gerbils are enjoying some out-of-cage time. Important: keep an eye on the agile acrobats so that no harm comes to them.

soon figure out what you're up to and will try—more quickly with each attempt—to scamper away the moment you come near them. They don't want to be put back in their cage! Locked up once more, they first set off on a brief inspection tour, just to make sure that everything is in order in their home territory. After that, however, they rarely move on to the day's business. Instead, they first show their displeasure at being back inside by taking it out on their cage: They scratch on the walls, burrow in the corners, and gnaw on the wires—just as if they wanted to escape again as quickly as possible from the confines of their cage.

Amusement Park for Gerbils

Exercise wheel

A wooden exercise wheel designed to be safe for gerbils, like this one, won't be accepted by all animals right away. Always offer it to them, though, as one of many attractive activities to choose from.

Hayrack

A hayrack for these steppe animals also functions as "exercise equipment." They'll pick up hay from the floor, too, but the extra effort involved in getting it out of the rack gives them some additional activity.

Cardboard tubes

Cardboard tubes, like those left over from paper towels or toilet paper, automatically belong to the gerbils! Some behavioral biologists even refer to the gerbils' enthusiasm for tubes as a sort of "tunnel mania": Wherever there's a tube, the gerbil "must" crawl in. Tubes like this don't last long, though. They are quickly chewed up into bedding—also a form of activity for gerbils!

Twigs

Twigs from nontoxic woody plants are excellent toys for keeping gerbils busy. As far as the animals' passion for gnawing is concerned, they can indulge themselves to their heart's content. You can offer bare winter twigs or else leafy ones.

Climbing equipment

Whether you provide built-in platforms in the cage or movable wooden roots, blocks, hanging bridges, and pieces of bark, the inquisitive rodents are sure to enjoy them. In order to keep the toys interesting for your gerbils, it's a good idea to rearrange them after each cage cleaning. Make sure they can't topple over, though, especially if there are young animals in the group!

Open areas

Make sure your Mongolian gerbils have enough open space to romp among the toys you've set up—as indicated here at the lower edge of the photo. These active animals like to wander from one interesting activity to the next. In between, however, they enjoy dashing around. They prefer to run along the wall rather than across an open area.

Safety During Out-of-Cage Time

Regardless of whether you enclose an area indoors for out-of-cage time or designate an entire room for it, it's important to ensure the safety of your little acrobats, and to do so before you let them out of the cage.

Eliminating Potential Hazards

During free-roaming time, there should be as few people as possible in the area, and they should not open doors to the room. That's because it's all too easy for the delicate extremities of the little creatures to get caught under a door or for somebody to step on one of them. If you have set up an enclosed play area in a room, then the walls of the enclosure should be at least 20 inches (50 cm) high because the gerbils can easily hop over lower

obstacles with a determined leap—especially if they get a running start or jump from an elevated spot nearby, like a toy. So be very careful.

› Electrical wires, even if they are unplugged, should not be left lying around because the gerbils can chew on them or bite through them. The same is true of any other objects left lying on the floor, such as newspapers, baskets, your knitting, or shoes.

› Put away everything gerbils could climb up on (like blankets on a sofa) or fall into (like vases).

› Close windows and doors (including tilting windows) through which the animals could escape. All the same, never let the animals out of your sight.

› Gerbils like to crawl under as well as behind furniture. From my own unfortunate experience, I know that the animals love to disappear behind books, where they will enthusiastically trim the pages. Getting them out again from behind the furniture is difficult. Therefore you should plan ahead and block access to hiding places like these, for instance, by placing a board in front of them. Never move a piece of furniture in order to get at an animal, though—it's too easy for you to injure him in the process!

› Flower pots within reach of the gerbils become a digger's paradise where they will eagerly tunnel into the potting soil and perhaps nibble on a leaf. Poisonous houseplants (see Internet addresses, page 62) are therefore taboo in the gerbil room.

› Other pets, like dogs or cats, should be banished from the room for the duration of the gerbils' out-of-cage time.

When carrying the gerbil, use your other hand to protect him. He'll quickly try to get his feet back on solid ground.

Running free outdoors: I strongly advise against this, because the agile rodents can quickly tunnel under the edge of the enclosure, climb over it, or jump it. Then they are lost forever.

Never Tug on the Tail!

In order to get an animal out of a hiding place or prevent him from running away, you might be tempted to hold tight to his tail. Please don't ever do that! And if you ever do inadvertently catch a gerbil by his tail, let go of it right away. Otherwise, you'll trigger a survival mechanism that the animals have in case a predator grabs them by the tail: The skin tears off completely! Because of your carelessness, the animal may escape with a skeletonized tail while you are left standing there, horror-stricken, holding the skin in your fingers. The exposed tailbone becomes necrotic and shrivels up, the dead tissue eventually falls off, and then the wound heals. However, because tail-slip, as this is called, involves a risk of infection, and it looks horrible besides, you should take the animal to a veterinarian if this ever happens. The veterinarian will remove the tailbone and take care of the wound.

What to Do When You're on Vacation

Even before you get your gerbils, you should think about finding someone to take care of the animals when you're away on vacation. Show the pet sitter how to carry out all routine tasks required in caring for the gerbils while you're on vacation as well as how to handle the animals properly. Make sure you are well stocked with everything the animals will need during your absence. Clean the cage thoroughly one last time before you leave in order to take some of the burden off the sitter.

Tips for the **Gerbil Sitter**

Use this checklist to show your pet sitter what to do while you're on vacation. This way the sitter can keep an eye on things.

FOOD	Specify the quantity and composition of the food, as well as when the animals are to be fed.
CLEANING	Explain how often the cage should be cleaned and what all this entails. If possible, let your pet sitter help you take care of the gerbils before you leave so that he/she can learn the necessary techniques.
BEHAVIOR	Describe the normal behavior of your animals. Point out warning signs, like those requiring a trip to the veterinarian.
INFORMATION	Have this manual handy as a quick reference; also provide your exact address during vacation, including fax and telephone numbers, as well as the contact information of a veterinarian your pet sitter can go to in an emergency.
IMPORTANT	Don't demand too much of the pet sitter: If he/she doesn't like the idea of feeding live foods (like mealworms) or feels unsure about letting the animals have out-of-cage time, then it's better to skip these things while you're away. It won't do the gerbils any harm.

Introducing New Gerbils

At some point, you might buy a new gerbil to add to your group.

Introducing a new gerbil—how to make it work:

> For the most part, only young animals can be introduced to an existing group without much trouble.

> One male and one female or two males usually (but not always) form more stable pairs than two females.

> Take advantage of the fact that group members recognize each other by scent. This means that you should rub the new animal with some of the clan's soiled, strongly "scented" bedding before putting him in the cage.

> Try to introduce the gerbils to each other in a fairly large area, perhaps in a room during out-of-cage time. This way the strangers can meet, but they can also get away from each other. They'll also detect each other's scent marks in the area. Once the two begin to tolerate each other to some extent, you can start to shrink this area by

Gerbils are naturally social animals that live in family groups consisting of parents and their offspring from one or two litters. Introducing new gerbils to each other isn't always successful or long lasting.

fencing off part of it so that the animals encounter each other more frequently. This way you push them gradually toward the open cage. If the introduction is successful, they will soon both make use of it.

> Place the two unacquainted gerbils in a small cage measuring about 12 × 12 inches (30 × 30 cm) that you have divided in half with a wire mesh partition. The animals should be able to sniff each other through the mesh, but not bite each other. Twice a day, switch the gerbils to each other's territory and rub them with the other's bedding. After one week, remove the partition and test whether the gerbils remain peaceful. If they don't, continue the described procedure for a few more days and then test their behavior again without the partition. If the animals get along, which you must continue to monitor, they should remain together for another week in the small cage minus partition. Afterward, move them into a somewhat larger cage, for example, 20 × 12 inches (50 × 30 cm), where they will again remain for about two or three weeks. Only then can you put the pair in a "normal" gerbil cage measuring about 32 × 12 inches (80 × 30 cm). There's a reason for this procedure: If you put the animals in large cage too soon, the fact that it is so spacious means that encounters occur there less frequently, which results in the animals becoming estranged again. That's why the cage you use for introductions should have only one floor!

Tip: Introducing gerbils to each other can succeed—but there's no guarantee that it will. These are independent animals with their own way of life, the details of which remain hidden from us. However, even with initially successful introductions, squabbles or even biting can develop later. If that happens, separate the animals immediately.

When Not to Introduce a New Gerbil

TIPS FROM
GERBIL EXPERT
Engelbert Kötter

In principle, gerbils should never be kept singly. They are gregarious animals with a strong need for close social contact. However, sometimes it's necessary to ignore this rule for practical reasons and keep just one gerbil.

DEATH OF THE PARTNER If one partner in an older pair dies, then it is not a good idea to replace him (or her) with a young animal. The older animal is nearing the end of his life; after his death, the younger animal will be alone again, and you'll have to introduce another gerbil—which, as already mentioned, doesn't always work. In this way you create an ongoing problem.

INCOMPATIBILITY If you have to remove one animal from an existing group because he (or she) bites or is bitten by others, you should avoid the stress of keeping him with a completely unfamiliar animal. It's better, then, to house him with another animal from the original group, one known to get along with the outcast gerbil.

Husbandry and Health Care

A balanced, varied diet—one that also provides activity for the animals—and proper husbandry are the two fundamental requirements for a long, healthy life for your gerbils. It is especially rewarding to take care of gerbils and be a part of their life right from the day of their birth.

Healthy Diet

As part of a balanced diet, carbohydrates, proteins, and fats as well as water, vitamins, and minerals are needed to maintain healthy, energetic gerbils. Wild Mongolian gerbils feed mainly on the seeds of grasses and other herbaceous plants as well as the occasional insect. They also dig up plant roots and eat them.

What Gerbils Like to Eat

For our pets, we can maximize their nutrition and health by starting with a good base food and adding fresh foods.

Pellets: This is their primary food and can be left in the cage, available at all times. Good quality rodent chow or lab block can be purchased at pet stores or may be ordered through Internet sites. You should purchase as much as you will use in a three-month period in order to maintain the quality of the food. Rodent chow should have a protein content of 16 percent or more and a 4–5 percent fat content. These commercial foods are complete diets properly balanced for your gerbil's needs and should comprise about 90 percent of your gerbil's diet. A healthy gerbil eats about 0.2 to 0.3 oz (5.7 to 8.5 g) of dry food per day. Note: If a very young gerbil has trouble eating this hard food, it is okay to soften the food in water for a few weeks until your gerbil can handle the hard product.

Grains, nuts, and seeds: Nuts and seeds are well loved by gerbils; they usually eat them preferentially. While they make a great treat and supplement for your special charge, the high fat content of these foods make them unsuitable as a predominant part of the diet. Limit nuts and seeds to just a few per day as a special treat. A small amount of grass seed packaged as a gerbil diet can be given daily, but sunflower seeds, pumpkin seeds, and peanuts should be given only occasionally. Small amounts of cooked pasta or hard bread can also be fed.

Protein: Your gerbil will get sufficient protein from his commercial diet. You can add mealworms, crickets, plain yogurt, or cottage cheese in small amounts with the fresh food portion of the diet. Any uneaten dairy products must be removed within a few hours so that spoiled food does not sit in the cage.

Fruits and Vegetables: When you clean vegetables, you can give the leftover scraps to your pets. For example, carrot peels, green peppers, and leafy lettuces including endive and chicory would provide scraps that make ideal offerings. Remove any fresh foods that your gerbils haven't eaten by the following day, then adjust the amount you feed them accordingly.

Supplements: If you feed your gerbils a balanced diet as described, supplements like vitamins or minerals will not be necessary. They are found in adequate amounts in the commercial food you provide as well as the fruits, vegetables, and seeds you offer.

Feeding Properly

› As long as your gerbils' diet is, on the whole, balanced and varied, it doesn't matter if they occasionally get too much or too little of one or another of the essential nutrients. Even on nature's menu, the quantities of food on hand for animals in the wild would vary from day to day. Keep in mind, though, that not all gerbils have the same dietary requirements: Active pups can tolerate a more energy-rich diet with higher levels of fat and protein than older animals that may already be over-weight. In addition, both pregnant and nursing females need a diet that contains significantly more protein and vitamins than the rest of the pets you keep.

› Give the daily food ration in several small portions rather than all at once. If you feed larger quantities, some of it will occasionally be left over and go to waste because the animals either could not or would not eat everything you offer. Gerbils are actually picky eaters. If they are allowed to choose, they will eat their favorite foods first, for example sunflower seeds and peanuts, and keep going until they are full. Foods they are less fond of would simply be left behind, uneaten.

For gerbils as for people, though, a balanced diet is what matters most. Only when you are feeding enough to last for several days, perhaps for a long weekend, is it advisable to give extra rations. For my animals, giving extra rations simply means that the water bottle is freshly filled and there is only as much fresh food as is sure to be eaten in one or two days. In this case, contrary to my usual practice, I would instead put the rodent chow in a bowl to prevent it from being buried in the

Insects as Live Food

Mongolian gerbils enjoy eating insects. Of course, you can catch them yourself in your house or yard, but it's a good idea to check out the terrarium section of your pet store. There you'll find live foods that are suitable for gerbils, like mealworms, crickets, or grasshoppers.

FRESH FOODS Fruits and vegetables, especially root vegetables like carrots, parsnips, or parsley root, provide vitamins and minerals; they are also a good way to supply these steppe animals with additional moisture. Because not all gerbils are eager to drink from a water bottle, this makes moist foods all the more important. However, the animals' digestive system is not adapted to handle too much fresh food, and an animal can develop diarrhea in response to it. This means you have to feed the correct amount with proper supervision.

RODENT CHOW It's not necessary to give gerbils a bowl for their food, because they'll eat their food right from the ground. However, it helps you learn to gauge how much of each food the animals actually eat per day. This information is useful, especially when you are trying to switch to a new food. Use a container that won't tip over when a gerbil stands on its edge!

PROTEINS Most gerbils like to eat insects (or, as a substitute, plain yogurt, cottage cheese, or hard-boiled egg yolks). They are especially important for pregnant and nursing females.

bedding. However, if pups are being nursed in the cage, I try to avoid feeding several days' worth of rations all at once so that I can keep an eye on the animals.

Food for Fun

It is fun to watch these steppe animals as they rummage around industriously in the bedding, searching for their dry food, and then as they twist and turn it between their front paws, open the shells deftly with their sharp teeth, and finally eat the fruit of their labors. Keep in mind, though, that food for your gerbils serves not just a nutritional function; it also plays an important role in keeping them busy and active. If gerbils have to look for their food and don't simply have it served to them in a bowl, they are happier and more relaxed. Animals that eat too much, get too little exercise, and have too little to do quickly become obese.

Therefore, instead of putting their food into a bowl, simply scatter it around on the bedding. The gerbils will find it there as they hunt and dig

around, and will gain satisfaction from their successful endeavors.

Water for Steppe Animals

Gerbils in the wild are known to quench their thirst by licking up the morning dew. Each animal consumes 0.1 to 0.2 ounce (3 to 5 ml) of water per day, but of course nursing females will drink more. Fresh water, then, belongs on your gerbils' menu—even if some of them would rather eat fresh foods than drink water. Don't be surprised if your gerbils don't accept the water bottle. Youngsters seem to learn how to use a bottle like this from their mother. If she comes from a line that is used to water bottles, she will pass this learned behavior on to her offspring. If the gerbils don't accept water, you can easily compensate for this with fresh foods—you should still offer water, though. Gerbils, by the way, have a special trick on tap: They can obtain water from the metabolic breakdown of fat.

A gerbil must first retrieve her treats from a cache of food like this one.

Healthy Food – Longer Life

Unlike their wild relatives, pet gerbils cannot pick and choose their food themselves from nature's bounty. That's why you must regularly offer them a diet that is balanced, healthy, varied, and low in fat.

Helpful

+ Seeds of grasses and other herbaceous plants are the main food of wild Mongolian gerbils. The food you select should be a balanced rodent chow based on this nutritional background.

+ Pregnant and nursing female gerbils need additional protein in their diet. You can provide it with hard-boiled egg yolks and insects like flies, crickets, or mealworms.

+ Nutritious foods include weeds like dandelion, plantain, and chickweed. Collect these plants only from clean, unpolluted sites, though—not along roadsides.

Harmful

− If you feed your gerbils cereals, avoid the sweetened mixtures. Sugar is bad for the animals' teeth and digestion.

− Don't leave the food in open packages; instead, keep it dry and stored in tightly sealed containers. It mustn't get moldy.

− Don't overdo it when feeding fruits and vegetables, because these steppe dwellers should get fresh foods as a supplement to their diet, not as their primary food.

− It's better not to feed raw beans or cabbage. The former are poisonous, while the latter is difficult to digest.

Cleaning the Gerbil Cage

Gerbils are very clean animals, and their cage must be kept clean, as well. When properly cared for, gerbils do not have an unpleasant odor. It also helps that they produce very little urine and relatively dry feces.

What has to be done?

It's enough if you remove the most obvious dirt, like deposits of droppings, once a week. That's an easy task because there is plenty of bedding in the cage, and the gerbils are always shredding new material to add to it. If there's an accidental spill, for instance, if the water bottle leaks, then you have to remove the damp bedding, otherwise it will get moldy. You can also prevent mold and decay by removing uneaten fruit and vegetables. Take them away after one or two days, before they start to spoil. You can leave leftover herbaceous plants or

When gerbils groom each other, this fosters cleanliness as well as social contact within the group. In the process, they exchange scents, which the clan members use to recognize each other.

the seed heads of grasses, provided they have dried and turned to hay. They are also eaten or chewed up when dry.

Cleaning the cage thoroughly: This is only necessary about once a month, depending on the size of the cage and the number of animals in the group. If the cage hasn't been cleaned in four to six weeks, though, or if the upper levels of the cage, the ramps leading up to them, or the tunnels of a multi-unit cage system are dirty, then the smell may become a real problem!

To begin a thorough cage cleaning, catch and remove the gerbils, but not with your hand; instead, use a cardboard tube (see page 37), then put the animals in a secure temporary cage like a travel carrier. If you have a multi-unit cage system, simply send the little creatures into a neighboring cage.

Dump the old bedding in the trash. Thoroughly wash the emptied glass tank or the bottom tray as well as washable accessories like connecting tunnels and resting platforms, but not the toys (exercise wheel, roots, or branches), using hot, clear water—don't use cleaners, though, because of the smell.

Disinfection: You usually don't have to disinfect the equipment. This is only necessary if an animal was sick and the illness was caused by bacteria or viruses. Your veterinarian will give you detailed advice about this. You can get suitable disinfectants at the pet store. Use these products only as directed. After treating any equipment with disinfectant, you always have to rinse it off with hot water. As soon as the cage and accessories are dry, put in the bedding (see page 28), and then set up the gerbils' cozy home again.

Gerbil Care **Schedule**

Here you can see at a glance what needs to be done:

DAILY	Make sure all animals are present and healthy. Is the gerbil cage locked securely? Has there been any change in the cage that would jeopardize your animals' safety and require you to take action? Don't forget to feed the animals and provide material to gnaw on.
WEEKLY	Remove the most obvious dirt. If necessary, replenish the animals' bedding and put in additional nest-building materials. Clean the water bottles thoroughly and refill them with fresh water. Let the agile rodents have one or two hours of out-of-cage time in their play area.
MONTHLY	Thoroughly clean the cage and accessories.
AS NEEDED	Special cleaning and disinfection are necessary only if a gerbil had an infectious disease. Be especially attentive if a gerbil is pregnant or has pups in the nest, or if squabbles break out in the group or between two animals during the introduction phase. Then you may have to intervene and separate the animals.

Health Care

If Mongolian gerbils are given the care and feeding this species requires, they are not very susceptible to disease. Like all pets, though, they can get sick. Their life expectancy is usually three years. Older gerbils do get sick more often, especially from age-related cancers, which frequently cause their death (see page 55).

To monitor the health of your gerbils, weigh the animals with a letter scale if you notice any dramatic change in their weight. An adult female weighs about 2.5 to 3.5 ounces (70 to 100 g), an adult male about 2.8 to 3.5 ounces (80 to 100 g), or 3.9 ounces (110 g) at most. If the animals are overweight or underweight, check their diet and make any necessary adjustments. In case of underweight, you could feed more sunflower seeds, for example; for overweight, on the other hand, cut back on the high-fat foods in favor of more grains (see page 46). Also make sure you are giving your gerbils enough opportunity for exercise inside the cage (exercise wheel, multi-cage system) as well as outside (free-roaming time).

Quick Checkup

Whenever you are holding your gerbils in your hands (see page 37), give them a quick checkup:

This little critter is the picture of gerbil health: agile and alert!

Scratching is a normal part of grooming. Excessive scratching, however, requires your attention.

❯ Are the four incisors in the upper and lower jaws still intact (see page 11)? Check to see that they overlap properly so they can wear each other down—after all, they grow continuously.

❯ Is there anything unusual about the nails; for instance, are they causing crooked toes (see page 56)?

❯ Is the anal area clean, or is it smeared with feces (see page 55)?

The large scent gland on the gerbil's abdomen, which is normally a comparatively bare spot in the middle of the belly, often looks dirty. The hair around it can appear matted because gerbils rub this gland on prominent features in their territory in order to scent-mark them with the gland's secretion. The surrounding hairs also become covered with this secretion, but there's nothing unusual about that. Males mark more often than females.

You can check the weight of your gerbils using a bowl and a household scale—providing, of course, you are fast enough. . . .

First Signs of Illness

In addition to examining animals up close like this, you can also tell whether or not they are doing well if you take a look at them when you pass by the cage. Healthy and energetic gerbils are agile animals that investigate their surroundings and participate actively in the life of the clan. Sickly animals are unwilling to enter the nest, stay away from the group, and may sleep alone outside the nest. They usually sit hunched over and keep their eyes closed. The coat is not smooth and soft, but rough and unkempt with straggly tufts of hair. Animals like this demand your attention because they might need your help. A scruffy coat can indicate malnutrition, illness, or a parasite infestation. However (and this is far more often the case),

it can also be due merely to relatively high environmental humidity, which can be the case during rainy weeks in the summer or in rooms with lots of water vapor (for instance a steamy kitchen, a room housing several aquariums, or a cold and damp cellar). Then you have to move the animals' cage to a drier, warmer spot (see page 23). If the scruffy gerbil is as lively as ever, you should still keep an eye on her, but with proper husbandry conditions (be sure to monitor these) and with no further signs of illness, you needn't be seriously concerned about her.

The same holds true if a gerbil scratches occasionally. However, if the animal's scratching is exceptionally frequent and prolonged, a parasite or fungus could be to blame (see page 56).

The Most Common Health Problems

It has been my experience that gerbils are relatively robust and insensitive to pain. After a painful incident (like a wasp sting or an accidental fall without serious consequences), they recover very quickly. It is especially amazing that if a gerbil is in pain—for example, after being bitten during a serious fight with a cage mate—she withdraws into one corner of the cage (she doesn't go immediately to the others in the nest!), and then other clan members often come and "comfort" her. When they do this, they hold their heads very close to the sick animal, which then squeaks.

If you suspect a gerbil is sick, keep an especially close eye on her. If the suspicion of illness is confirmed, then proceed carefully and resolutely in order to come to the animal's aid. Remain calm

An infrared lamp helps a sick gerbil stay warm when she is separated from her cage mates and can't snuggle with them.

and deliberate, even with serious problems like tail-slip (see page 41).

Leave a sick gerbil with her clan, unless you have to separate the animals because of biting or at the recommendation of your veterinarian. This is because even after a brief absence, a gerbil may no longer smell "right" (see page 8) and could be expelled from the group!

Gerbils with potentially contagious disorders, whether parasitic, fungal, or bacterial and usually evidenced through skin changes, diarrhea, or eye or respiratory problems, must be isolated. A potentially contagious or known contagious gerbil should be housed separately. Gloves should be worn for handling and cage cleaning and hands immediately washed when done. Gloves should be discarded and not reused. You must not transfer anything from the isolation ward to the everyday habitat.

When to go to the veterinarian: If you don't know whether your gerbil is sick or with what, you should definitely go to a veterinarian. Not every veterinarian treats gerbils. Call your local veterinarian and inquire. If your local veterinary practice does not treat gerbils, they can refer you to a practice that does. Large specialty practices and those associated with veterinary schools commonly treat gerbils. Many veterinary practices have Web sites. A quick look may tell which types of patients each practice sees.

Caring for a Sick Gerbil

If your gerbil is sick, make sure she has everything she needs. If necessary, provide a little additional

Recognizing Health Problems in Gerbils

SYMPTOMS	CAUSES	TREATMENT
Trembling, unsteadiness, severe shaking	**Seizure:** Up to 40% of gerbils develop seizures beginning at approximately two months of age and usually decreasing with age. Individual seizures can be precipitated by stress or loud noises.	Stay calm. Intervene only if your gerbil is in a dangerous spot during the seizure, for example, on a platform or next to a water bowl. In this case, move your gerbil to a location without hazards. Avoid loud noises and stress. No other treatment is necessary.
Skeletonized tail ("tail-slip")	**Carelessness:** The animal was grabbed by the tail, causing the skin to slip off the tailbone.	Go to the veterinarian, who will amputate the tail and treat the wound.
Sore nose, hair loss on face, red areas on face	**Nasal and/or facial dermatitis:** This can be caused by unsanitary conditions, excessive humidity, or aggressive burrowing inducing a *staphylococcal* infection.	Mild cases may resolve with improvement of the living conditions. Severe cases require veterinary care and antibiotics.
Coughing, nasal discharge, red tears, unusual breathing noises	**Environmental problems** including a drafty cage, cold room, high humidity, and overheating; medical problems including pneumonia, common in gerbils.	Improve housing and environmental conditions; veterinary treatment for pneumonia.
Soft feces in cage: Gerbils have a wet tail stained with fecal matter.	Wet tail is caused by any **intestinal problem** that results in diarrhea. Commonly, it is an inflammation or infection of the intestines caused by nematodes (worms) or protozoa. It can also be caused by improper diet.	Have your gerbil and a fecal sample evaluated by a veterinarian to determine treatment.
Lumps and swellings, especially in the abdominal area	**Tumors and cancer** are common in gerbils. The most frequent types are cancer of the ovaries, skin, ventral scent gland, and of the mammary glands. Cancer is more common in older gerbils.	Consult with your veterinarian regarding surgical removal of any masses.
Apathetic animal, rapid physical decline	**Tyzzer's disease:** The most dangerous bacterial disease affecting gerbils.	Antibiotic therapy by the veterinarian.

warmth for the animal by using an infrared lamp. Check the distance between the animal (or the bedding) and the lamp, though, so that the dry bedding doesn't catch fire. For the animal, the temperature under the lamp should be about 77°F (25°C). Do not leave a lamp like this burning overnight unattended.

You can solve some problems yourself:

› Bite wounds, when they are fresh and bloody, look especially bad. They can occur during fights among gerbils that are competing for rank in the clan. The areas primarily affected are the muzzle, the base of the tail, and the back. Separate the animals (see back flap) to protect the victimized gerbil from being bitten again. The wounds themselves

---

When a **Pet Dies**

SAYING GOOD-BYE The loss of a beloved animal is a serious matter for children, especially if they were very close to their pet and/or this is their first experience of death. This situation calls for great sensitivity on the part of the parents. Of course, you have to be careful that the dead animal doesn't become a health hazard. But you also have to make sure that the children have enough time to deal with their grief. In such cases, doing something like burying the animal in your own garden is not only legal, but it's also an important ritual for saying good-bye.

COMING TO TERMS WITH A PET'S DEATH If you allow your gerbils to have offspring (see page 58), it may be easier to accept the death of individual animals. Alternatively, you can bring home new gerbils.

---

usually heal quickly on their own. Check to see if any of them becomes inflamed, though, and in this case go to the veterinarian.

› You can also remedy crooked toes due to overgrown nails yourself. This condition develops when the gerbils don't wear down their ever-growing "toenails" enough as they walk around. You can help them improve nail wear by covering the bottom of the cage with enough sand for them to scratch around in (see page 29). For the time being, reduce the depth of the upper layer of bedding so that the animals can run and dig more in the sand. In addition, give the affected animals more and longer out-of-cage time on rough tile floors.

› You have to be careful when you trim their nails. Clip off just the tip of the overgrown nail! Caution: The actual toe of the animal lies hidden in the nail, and it takes experience for you to be able to recognize it; even then you can't always be certain if the nails are horn colored and semitransparent. With dark-colored nails, you can't see the toes showing through. That's why the rodents' toes are frequently nicked when their nails are trimmed. If you are unsure of yourself, have an expert show you the correct way to trim nails! Or let the veterinarian do it.

› Gerbils sometimes scratch themselves long and hard with their claws. It looks as if they are doggedly trying to get at those hard-to-reach spots on their body. If you observe this sort of behavior, then check the animals for parasites or skin problems. While both can be spread by natural means and arise spontaneously, your gerbils may also have been infected by other animals. Parasites or infections can be introduced even by transferring infected accessories from one cage to another,

Observers have often seen gerbils come over to a sick companion and put their heads next to the ailing animal, as if to comfort her.

When giving vitamins, it's easiest to sprinkle them on grains or flakes of food, then spoon-feed them; this way you can control the dosage.

such as when playing with gerbils that have come to visit. Have the veterinarian diagnose parasites, such as mites. Treat them with medications from the veterinarian or pet store, following the instructions for product use. You'll have to disinfect the cage and its furnishings, as well.

Be Careful Here

› If the gerbil's scratching is associated with festering wounds, this can indicate a staphylococcal infection. Don't allow these pus-forming bacteria to get into a wound!

› Inflamed bald patches in the gerbil's coat, if they are temporary, may be nothing to worry about. However, if they last for several days and spread, they may be due to ringworm. This is a skin fungus that can also infect humans. If you seriously suspect contagious infections of this sort (for example,

conjunctivitis; see Table, page 55; staphylococcus; ringworm), observe the strictest hygiene. In any case, see a veterinarian for a diagnosis. If you fear that you have been infected yourself, you must consult your family doctor right away.

At the End of Life

About 80 percent of all pet gerbils live for two to four years. Of the rest, approximately equal numbers die sooner or live longer.

After years of friendship with a gerbil, it is difficult to have to say good-bye as your pet's life draws to a close. In a previously healthy gerbil, one indication that the end is near is sudden weight loss. The gerbil is less able to get around, staggers weakly around the cage, and often sits there apathetically, scarcely eating, until death arrives.

Reproduction in Gerbils

Watching gerbils rear their young is fascinating—especially if the cage is in a warm room, because then the mother opens up the nest and it's easy to see the babies ("pups"). The mother often starts by licking the pups clean, then she hunches over them to suckle them. The pups lie on their back and fight over the nipples, especially if there are more than eight hungry mouths competing for their mother's milk. They drum on the mother's breast with their front paws to stimulate the flow of milk. When the pups are older but still blind, they keep trying to crawl out of the nest. The mother uses her teeth to grab the pup by a lengthwise fold of skin—not by the scruff of the neck, as with other animals—and carries it back to the nest. If you decide to observe this for yourself and allow your gerbils to reproduce, keep in mind that this will increase the size of your gerbil colony. Usually only the highest-ranking pair in the clan breeds, but occasionally there are exceptions. In time you will need several cages for your gerbils' offspring, or neighbors willing to provide homes for each new litter. If you do not separate the males and females, the gerbils can easily form a colony of about twenty animals. The danger of fighting and biting among rivals increases with clan size.

Breeding Your Gerbils

Breeding pets is a serious undertaking. It often changes your relationship with your gerbils from a caretaker-pet relationship to a caretaker-breeding stock relationship. The responsibilities are significant. Not only must you provide extra care and attention to the breeding females, you must be prepared to house and care for all the progeny, including establishing separate clans when your first clan reaches an antisocial size. If you will not be able to care for all the

1 NEST To build the nest in time for the birth of her pups, the mother needs plenty of nesting material like tissue paper and hay.

2 PUPS After giving birth, the mother needs rest in order to adjust to the new situation. She also needs more protein in her diet. After a few days, you can check on the pups.

3 CARRYING If a mother gerbil has accepted her young, she will retrieve a pup that has crawled out of the nest.

gerbils yourself, you must arrange alternate homes in advance of breeding. Breeding should not be undertaken if your primary intent is a bonded gerbil pet.

To breed your gerbils, use only adult animals that are not aggressive and have shown no tendency towards epileptic seizures. It's best if the animals are about the same age and get along well. It is even a good idea to select especially friendly and intelligent animals for the purpose, because to some extent parental characteristics like these are inherited by the young. Males reach sexual maturity about 70 to 85 days after birth, the females in about 65 to 85 days.

The gestation period is normally 23 to 26 days. If the mother gerbil is already nursing a litter, however, then the birth can be postponed for about another 20 days. It is always an unmistakable sign that birth is imminent when the female withdraws from the clan and moves into a nest. Either the mother-to-be or the clan builds a new nest. The pups, usually three to eight in number, come into the world naked, blind, and deaf. Five days after birth, the ears open; the eyes open when the pups are 18 to 23 days old. The fur begins to grow by the sixth day, and around the twelfth day the teeth appear. The mother suckles the pups for 21 to 30 days, until they weigh about 1 to 2 ounces (30 to 60 g) and begin to eat on their own. At about five to six weeks of age, the pups are capable of surviving on their own, but they shouldn't be separated from the clan until seven to eight weeks at the earliest, because during this period they learn important social behavior.

Preventing Pregnancy

The only way to prevent postpartum pregnancy of a mother gerbil is to separate her from the male before she gives birth. Mating can usually take place again immediately after birth!

Problems **Raising Pups**

TIPS FROM
GERBIL EXPERT
Engelbert Kötter

As a rule, raising a litter of gerbil pups proceeds smoothly, with practically no help from the owner. All you have to do is keep an eye on things. In rare cases, problems can arise. (Although uncommon, if a pup is rejected, you must be prepared to foster the pup to another nursing mother or hand-feed the pup. Hand-feeding is often unrewarding but should be attempted by bottle feeding small amounts of KMR [kitten milk replacer] every couple of hours or trying bread soaked in evaporated milk.)

MOTHER GERBIL EATS HER OWN YOUNG
When the mother suffers from protein deficiency and doesn't produce enough milk for her pups, she instinctively reduces the size of her litter or even cannibalizes them all.

HOW TO PREVENT IT As birth approaches, give pregnant females more protein in their diet until the pups are weaned. If this happens to a female a second time despite getting enough protein, you cannot rely on this animal's instincts. She is unsuitable for breeding. Separate her from the breeding group and house her with a compatible young female, apart from the males.

L

legs, 9
lemmings, 7
life expectancy, 13
Lilac gerbils, 15

M

martens, 7
mice, 7, 13
Mongolia, 6
Muridae order, 7

N

natural habitat, 6–7, 11
nesting material, 26, 27, 58
nocturnal habits, 13
nose, 10, 15, 22, 55

O

odor, 12
offspring, 8, 58–59
ostracism, 20
owls, 7

P

parrots, 13
pellets, 45
pet stores, 14, 21, 22
playpen, 36
popularity, 4, 5
predators, 7, 13, 41

R

rabbits, 13
rats, 7, 13

S

reproduction, 58–59
Rodentia order, 7

S

safety, 40–41
saliva, 8
scent function, 7, 8, 10, 16, 42
seizures, 55
sexual organs, 20, 22
Siamese gerbils, 15
sleeping, 13
social structure, 8, 16–17, 20
soles, 11
spatial reasoning, 9, 17, 36
Spotted gerbils, 15

T

tail, 5, 8, 15, 17, 37, 41, 55
taming, 31–32
teeth, 11, 16, 22, 53
transportation, 21, 22
twigs, 39
Tyzzer's disease, 55

V

vacation caretaker, 12, 41
veterinarian, 13, 51, 54, 62
vision, 9, 10
voles, 7

W

water bottle, 26, 27, 48
whiskers, 9, 10

Organizations

> American Society for the Prevention of Cruelty to Animals (ASPCA)
424 E. 92nd Street
New York, NY 10128-6804
212-876-7700
www.aspca.org
> Humane Society of the United States (HSUS)
2100 L Street, NW
Washington, DC 20037
202-452-1100
www.hsus.org

To Find Veterinarians in Your Area

> Veterinarians.com
www.veterinarians.com
> Yextvets
www.yext.com/vets

Important Information

> Sick Gerbils If signs of illness appear in your gerbils, consult a veterinarian as soon as possible.

> Risk of Infection Only a few animal diseases can be transmitted to humans. If you suspect you have been infected, go to the doctor; this is especially true if you have been bitten by an animal.

> Animal Dander Allergy Many people have an allergic reaction to animal dander. If you aren't sure, ask your family doctor before buying any gerbils.

To Find Veterinarians Who Use Natural Remedies

> American Holistic Veterinary Medical Association
www.ahmva.org

To Find a Veterinary Hospital in Your Area

> The American Animal Hospital Association's "Healthypet.com"
http://healthypet.aahanet.org

Gerbils on the Internet

> The American Gerbil Society
www.agsgerbils.org
> National Gerbil Society
www.gerbils.co.uk
> "The Gerbils Color Palette"
http://home.wtal.de/ehr/gerbils/colors.htm
> "Gerbil Coat Colour Reference Guides"
www.egerbil.com/colours.html

Husbandry and Health Care

> American Animal Hospital Association's "Healthypet.com"
www.healthypet.com
> The Merck Veterinary Manual Online
www.merckvetmanual.com

Information on Poisonous Plants

ASPCA's "Animal Poison Control Center"
888-426-4435
www.aspca.org/pet-care/poison-control

HSUS's "Common Poisonous Plants"
www.hsus.org/pets/pet_care/protect_your_pet_from_common_household_dangers/common_poisonous_plants.html

Pet Sitters

> National Association of Professional Pet Sitters
856-439-0324
www.petsitters.org
> Pet Sitters International
336-983-9222
www.petsit.com

Books

> Anastasi, Donna. *Gerbils: The Complete Guide to Gerbil Care (Complete Care Made Easy)*. BowTie Press, Irvine, California, 2005.
> Fox, Sue. *Gerbils* (Animal Planet Pet Care Library). T.F.H. Publications, Neptune, New Jersey, 2007.
> Kahn, Cynthia M. (editor). *The Merck/Merial Manual for Pet Health, Home Edition*. Merck & Co., Inc., Whitehouse Station, New Jersey, 2007.
> Kötter, Engelbert. *My Gerbil and Me (For the Love of Animals)*. Barron's Educational Series, Inc., Hauppauge, New York, 2005.

Magazines

> *Critters USA*. Fancy Publications, Inc., Irvine, California.

The title of the German book is *Rennmäuse*
English Translation by Mary Lynch

All inquiries should be addressed to:
Barron's Educational Series, Inc.
250 Wireless Boulevard
Hauppauge, NY 11788
www.barronseduc.com

ISBN-13: 978-0-7641-4429-5
ISBN-10: 0-7641-4429-4

Library of Congress Catalog Card No.: 2009033314

Library of Congress Cataloging-in-Publication Data
Kötter, Engelbert.
   [Rennmäuse. English]
   Gerbils / Engelbert Kötter ; photographer, Christine Steimer.
     p. cm.
   Includes bibliographical references and index.
   ISBN-13: 978-0-7641-4429-5 (alk. Paper)
   ISBN-10: 0-7641-4429-4 (alk. Paper)
  1. Mongolian gerbils as pets. I. Title.
SF459. G4K6813 2010
636.935'83—dc22
                      2009033314

PRINTED IN CHINA
9 8 7 6 5 4 3 2 1

The Author

Engelbert Kötter has been keeping gerbils for years. He began his involvement with the little rodents in 1984 and was instrumental in introducing gerbils to the pet trade in Germany. Since then he has focused his attention on gerbil-friendly husbandry methods and has published both books and magazine articles on the subject. Engelbert Kötter is a freelance journalist who writes on gardening and pet care.

The Photographer

Christine Steimer is a freelance photographer specializing in photography of pets and domestic animals. She works for international book publishers, specialty magazines, and advertising agencies. Ms. Steimer provided all the photos in this book.

Acknowledgments

The author and publisher wish to thank the manufacturers of Elmato (*www.elmato.de*) and Marchioro (*www.marchioro.de*) brands for their kind support with products for the photo shoots.

SOS – What to Do?

The gerbil is gnawing on the cage wires

CAUSE The gerbil is bored, therefore she gnaws constantly on the cage wires. **THIS MIGHT HELP** Give the gerbil enough material to keep her busy with gnawing, nest building, exploring, or digging. You could also consider housing the gerbils in a glass tank.

A gerbil has escaped

CAUSE The cage was carelessly left unlocked, or it is damaged. **THIS MIGHT HELP** If the gerbil escaped indoors, put the opened cage where the gerbil can go back inside voluntarily. Try to lure the gerbil into a cardboard tube.

The gerbil is apathetic

CAUSE The animal is probably not feeling well. **THIS MIGHT HELP** Try to find out what has made the animal sick. In any case, take the gerbil to an experienced small-animal veterinarian, who will recommend the proper treatment. As much as possible, keep the sick animal warm and stress free.

Two gerbils are biting each other

CAUSE This could be an encounter between two gerbils that don't recognize each other. It can happen when a clan member no longer smells familiar because he has been away from the group for too long. Alternatively, one of the two could be a juvenile that wants to challenge an older animal for rank in the hierarchy. In larger groups, weak males and competing females can also be driven away by biting. **THIS MIGHT HELP** Separate the animals right away, being extremely careful not to get bitten yourself! A wire mesh partition is best for this purpose.

The gerbil scratches the ground constantly

CAUSE Digging around in the ground is normal; so-called stereotypical digging, however, especially in the corners of the cage, is an abnormal behavior. It is usually caused by boredom when the gerbil gets too little activity and there are no tunnels to explore. **THIS MIGHT HELP** You can decrease this behavior by providing a larger selection of toys, more materials to chew, and, above all, tunnels to crawl through.